Written by Diane Costa de Beauregard
Illustrated by Pierre de Hugo

Specialist adviser: Dr Jane Mainwaring,
The British Museum (Natural History)

ISBN: 1 85103 066 2
First published 1989 in the United Kingdom
by Moonlight Publishing Ltd,
131 Kensington Church Street, London W8
Translated by Penny Stanley-Baker

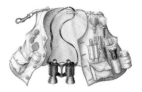

© *1988 by Editions Gallimard*
English text © *1989 by Moonlight Publishing Ltd*
Typeset in Great Britain by Saxon Printing Ltd., Derby
Printed in Italy by La Editoriale Libraria

POCKET • WORLDS

Wildlife Alert!

Do we really want to find ourselves on a lonely planet with nothing but farm animals to see?

The plants and animals we know today have developed over many millions of years, since life began on Earth. But now human beings are killing so many animals that whole species are being wiped out.

More animals disappear every year, for ever. **It is up to us to save the ones that are left.**

No one saved the dodo. It lived on the island of Mauritius, and was easy to catch because it couldn't fly. Two hundred years ago, the first sailors landed on the island, and began killing the dodos for fun. Now the dodo is extinct; there are none left at all.

Some old drawings give us an idea of what the dodo looked like, and this skeleton shows how big it was.

Crocodiles were there when dinosaurs ruled the Earth.

Are you afraid of crocodiles? It's true that some can be dangerous. But most crocodiles will only attack if they feel threatened. Crocodiles are often killed by fishermen, who say they eat all the fish. In fact, crocodiles eat dead and diseased meat, as well as live prey, so they help keep the water clean.

The Komodo dragon is another reptile which appeared in prehistoric times. It is no longer hunted, but it won't survive unless the animals it needs to eat are protected too.

Lots of crocodiles are shot so that people can make expensive handbags, shoes and wallets out of their skins. If this goes on, no crocodiles will be left. Shooting crocodiles is illegal, but that hasn't stopped poachers killing them. The Indian gavial, with its long thin snout and sharp teeth, is now so rare that it may soon die out and become extinct.

◀ Gavial

Plastic bags thrown into the sea look just like jellyfish. Soft-shelled turtles try to eat them, but the plastic chokes them and they die. ▶

Their first steps are sometimes their last!

When baby turtles hatch out of their eggs, they have to leave their sandy nests, and crawl all the way down the beach to the sea. They make a tasty meal for the birds which pick them off as they waddle along.

But enough turtles survive to have babies the next year.

But since people also began killing turtles, for their meat and eggs and for their beautiful shells, turtles have become much scarcer. Some are now raised on special farms, and released back into the wild, to breed.

Which is the biggest animal in the world?

The blue whale. Each year it swims all the way from the Arctic to the Antarctic and back again.

People have always hunted whales, not because they do any harm, but because there is a lot of meat on a whale, and thick layers of fat which can be made into oil.

Whales are very intelligent and sensitive animals. If a young whale is attacked, its mother will risk her own life to save her baby.

Modern whaling-ships with their rocket-fired harpoons have killed too many whales.

These clever, gentle creatures are becoming so scarce that many countries have stopped hunting them altogether. Why should we go on hunting them nowadays, when there are so few of them and we no longer need their meat?

Placid manatees like to take their time. They aren't quick enough to get out of the way when a boat comes by, and so they get hurt and die.

Why are so many water animals, such as monk seals, walrus, otters and manatees, becoming so scarce? Industrial waste and sewage have polluted the seas and rivers in which they live. Tourists disturb the peaceful waters where the animals rear their young, and the construction of dams makes many animals homeless.

Efforts are being made to repair the damage: many lakes are now nature reserves, and trees growing on the riverbank are preserved so that otters can raise their babies there.

Special centres have been set up on the shores of the North Sea, to rescue and care for motherless baby seals.

Who's afraid of the big, bad wolf?

Our fairy-tales are full of frightening stories about bears and wolves. They were hunted because they killed sheep, and because people were afraid of them.

There are no wolves left in Britain, but a few manage to survive in the wild, mainly in parts of central Europe and North America.

Brown bears left the plains and took to the hills when people began to hunt them. Out of the few bears left in Europe some live high up in the Pyrenees, far from any roads, where there is plenty of space for them to browse and play quietly, undisturbed by cars or people.

The snow leopard used to be hunted for its wonderful fur, but it is now extremely rare.

When one sort of animal disappears, the delicate balance of nature is disturbed.

The lynx used to play an important role in the forests of France, because it fed on chamois, the mountain goat. When the lynx disappeared, killed off by hunters, the chamois increased in number so much that they began to cause serious damage to the forests. Lynxes were reintroduced, but farmers shot them, because they were afraid they would eat their sheep!

Lynx ▶

The Siberian tiger, largest of all the great cats, has a very beautiful coat, but it is not for sale! Strict laws protect it in the Soviet Union, though not in China.

If this zebra, which is a herbivore, didn't have enough grass to eat, it would die …

People who hunt wild animals will probably disturb the balance of the food chain.

Game-wardens take wounded or sick animals to hospitals where they can be treated.

... and this cheetah, which is a carnivore, would have no prey to feed on.

Animal reserves have been set up all over the world in order to protect wildlife.

Once they have recovered, they are released back into the wild.

Killing elephants is against the law, but that doesn't stop people shooting them!

Elephants' tusks are made of ivory, which is carved into expensive ornaments and jewellery. If only people would stop buying these things, perhaps fewer elephants would be shot. The poachers don't kill just the adult elephants, they kill the babies too. When they die, there are no more elephants to take their place.

In parts of Africa, soldiers patrol the game reserves to try to protect the elephants, but despite all their efforts, more and more elephants are killed each year. If nothing is done, in twenty years' time the African elephant may be almost extinct.

The rhinoceros, too, is hunted for its horn, which is carved into dagger-handles. Powdered horn is also used as a medicine in parts of Asia. If the mother is killed the young baby will die too.

The bald eagle is the national emblem of the United States. At one time, so few of them remained that they were in danger of dying out altogether, but their numbers are now increasing. Other birds of prey, however, such as the condor, are now threatened with extinction unless more can be done to protect them.

Huge herds of bison and pronghorns once grazed on the

great North American prairies. The American Indians hunted them for food, but never killed more than they needed. Then came the European settlers. They wanted the land for their crops and cattle. Instead of killing a few animals at a time, they shot as many as they could; in just over a year Buffalo Bill killed 4,280 bison. Only a few of these great beasts escaped. Their descendants now live in the American National Parks, where they are safe.

Pronghorns

In many parts of the world, people are cutting down whole forests because they need the land to raise animals, or to grow crops to feed their families or to sell. But it means that the wild animals which lived in the forest have nowhere to go.

What is happening to the gorillas in the African rainforests?

There are hardly any left. Mother gorillas don't have more than one baby at a time. They only give birth every four or five years, so there are not enough baby gorillas to replace the ones that die. And yet people are still catching gorillas and using them for cruel scientific experiments!

Like the two gorillas on the left, this orang-outang lives in the tropical forest. All the great apes are losing their forest homes, and too many of them are being captured and put into zoos.

To help it survive, this aye-aye and others like it have been moved to a little island with plenty of trees, where no one will disturb them.

The panda is one of the rarest animals in the world.

It lives in the bamboo forests of China. Pandas need to eat at least 12 kilos of bamboo leaves and shoots each day to stay alive!

But the bamboo forests are being cut down. Bamboo grows for about sixty years before it flowers. Then it dies back, and doesn't produce any new shoots for another five years. If several parts of the bamboo forest die back at the same time, the pandas are left with nothing to eat.

Rescuing pandas from starvation.

When this happens, the Chinese save the pandas by moving them to another part of the forest where there is plenty of fresh, young bamboo for them to eat. These two men have drugged a panda and are carrying it along the slippery paths. Sometimes the pandas make the trip by helicopter.

Dead butterflies, sorted and ready for export.

Pictures like this are made from butterfly-wings.

Rare butterflies can be raised from chrysalides to help them survive.

The beautiful Morpho butterfly is a prize catch in the Amazonian forest.

Their bright colours make people want to catch them. Millions of butterflies are caught and sold each year. Lots of people collect them. Their wings are made into

pictures, paperweights and knick-knacks. Their numbers have decreased so much that special farms have been set up to raise butterflies and release them into the wild.

A few bustards still visit Britain from the Continent.

What has become of the bustards?

These turkey-like birds were once common in the fields, until farmers started to spray their crops and killed the plants bustards eat. Corncrakes used to nest amongst the reeds, but now most marshes have been drained, and the croak of the corncrake is hardly ever heard.

Corncrake

Are we doing enough to look after animals and plants?

Salmon lifts

Salmon swim upstream to lay their eggs each year. When dams are built the salmon can't get up them, so special ladders and lifts are often set up alongside the dam, to help the salmon on their way upstream.

As major rivers like the Thames are cleaned up, more and more salmon are put into them each year. But we shall have to fight hard against pollution if the salmon are to continue to breed!

1. The salmon find their way in.
2. They collect in the lift.
3. The lift tips them out higher up.
4. The salmon swim on upstream.

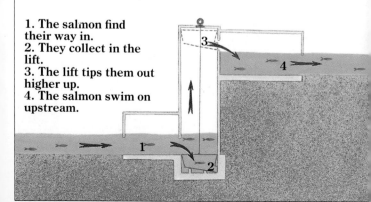

Are you a nature-lover? Then you'll want to take a closer look at the wildlife around you! You don't want to be seen, so don't wear bright colours. Crouch down low behind a bush or tree, and remember to keep quiet!

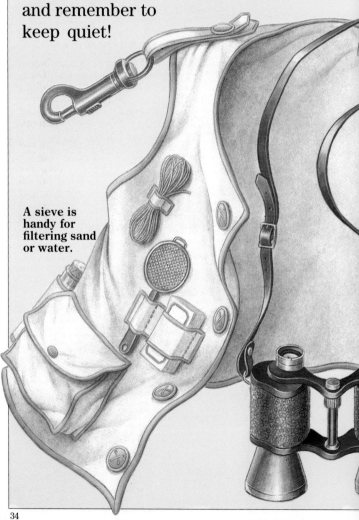

A sieve is handy for filtering sand or water.

When you are on the move, try to face into the wind, so that the animals don't hear you or catch your scent.

It's easier to carry your equipment on you than in a bag. Make yourself a special jacket with lots of pockets.

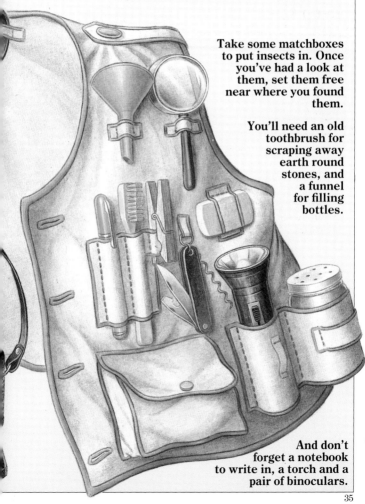

Take some matchboxes to put insects in. Once you've had a look at them, set them free near where you found them.

You'll need an old toothbrush for scraping away earth round stones, and a funnel for filling bottles.

And don't forget a notebook to write in, a torch and a pair of binoculars.

Index